VOCABULARY FOR
MARKETING
a workbook for users

by
Liz Greasby

PETER COLLIN PUBLISHING

First published in Great Britain 2000

Published by Peter Collin Publishing Ltd
1 Cambridge Road, Teddington, Middx, UK

British Library Cataloguing in Publication Data
A catalogue record for this book is available from the British Library

ISBN 1-901659-48-8

Text typeset by PCP Ltd
Printed by Nuffield Press, Oxfordshire, UK

Workbook Series
Check your:

Vocabulary for Banking and Finance	0-948549-96-3
Vocabulary for Business, 2nd edition	1-901659-27-5
Vocabulary for Colloquial English	0-948549-97-1
Vocabulary for Computing, 2nd edition	1-901659-28-3
Vocabulary for English	1-901659-11-9
Vocabulary for Hotels, Tourism, Catering	0-948549-75-0
Vocabulary for Law, 2nd edition	1-901659-21-6
Vocabulary for Marketing	1-901659-48-8
Vocabulary for Medicine, 2nd edition	1-901659-47-X

Specialist English Dictionaries

English Dictionary for Students	1-901659-06-2
Dictionary of Accounting	0-948549-27-0
Dictionary of Agriculture, 2nd edition	0-948549-78-5
Dictionary of American Business	0-948549-11-4
Dictionary of Automobile Engineering	0-948549-66-1
Dictionary of Banking & Finance	0-948549-12-2
Dictionary of Business, 2nd edition	0-948549-51-3
Dictionary of Computing, 3rd edition	1-901659-04-6
Dictionary of Ecology & Environment, 3rd edition	0-948549-74-2
Dictionary of Government & Politics, 2nd edition	0-948549-89-0
Dictionary of Hotels, Tourism, Catering	0-948549-40-8
Dictionary of Human Resources, 2nd edition	0-948549-79-3
Dictionary of Information Technology, 2nd edition	0-948549-88-2
Dictionary of Law, 3rd edition	1-901659-43-7
Dictionary of Library & Information Management	0-948549-68-8
Dictionary of Marketing, 2nd edition	0-948549-73-4
Dictionary of Medicine, 3rd edition	1-901659-45-3
Dictionary of Printing & Publishing, 2nd edition	0-948549-99-8
Dictionary of Science & Technology	0-948549-67-X

For details about our range of English and bilingual dictionaries and workbooks, please contact:

Peter Collin Publishing
1 Cambridge Road, Teddington, TW11 8DT, UK
tel: (+44) 020 8943 3386   fax: (+44) 020 8943 1673   email: info@petercollin.com
web site: **www.petercollin.com**

Introduction

The worksheets in this workbook contain a variety of exercises appropriate for students requiring a working knowledge of English marketing terminology. The worksheets can be used either for self-study or in the classroom and can be completed in any order. Several have 'extensions': short classroom exercises based on the language in the main exercise. All the questions within this workbook are based on the *Dictionary of Marketing, second edition* (published by *Peter Collin Publishing*, ISBN 0-948549-73-4).

This workbook is aimed at students with at least an intermediate level of English. However, many people who work in Marketing have to read in English on a regular basis; students with a more basic level of English may therefore already have the passive vocabulary to handle many of the exercises.

Specialist vocabulary
It is important to appreciate that 'knowing' specialist vocabulary involves more than simply recognising it.

- You can understand the meaning of a word when reading or listening and yet be unable to remember that same word when speaking or writing.
- You may remember the word, but use it incorrectly. This can be a grammatical problem, like knowing that 'import' can be used both as a noun and as a verb. Or it may be a question of collocation: we use *mail*-order, not *post*-order.
- Then there is the question of the sound of the word. Can you pronounce it? And do you recognise it when you hear it pronounced?

For these reasons - memory, use and sound - it is important that students practise specialist vocabulary so that they can learn to use it more confidently and effectively. The exercises in this workbook will help students to expand their knowledge and use of marketing vocabulary.

Photocopiable material
All the worksheets can be legally photocopied to use in class. If, as a teacher, you intend to use most of the book with a class you may find it more convenient for the students to buy a copy each. You are not allowed to photocopy or reproduce the front or back cover.

Using the *Dictionary of Marketing*
All of the vocabulary taught or practised in this workbook is in the Peter Collin Publishing *Dictionary of Marketing*. The *Dictionary of Marketing* gives definitions in simple English which students can read and understand. Many of the examples and definitions in the workbook are taken directly from the dictionary. Students should have a copy of the *Dictionary of Marketing* for referring to when completing the exercises; using the dictionary is an essential part of successful language learning.

Structure of a *Dictionary of Marketing* entry
Each entry within the dictionary includes key elements that help a student understand the definition of the term and how to use it in context. Each term has a clear example, and part of speech. This is followed by example sentences and quotations from newspapers and magazines that show how the term is used in real life. These elements of the dictionary are used to create the questions within this workbook.

Vocabulary Record Sheet
At the back of the book is a Vocabulary Record Sheet. Recording useful vocabulary in a methodical way plays a key role in language learning and could be done, for example, at the end of each lesson. The *Dictionary of Marketing* is a useful tool for ensuring that the personal vocabulary record is accurate and is a good source for example sentences to show how words are used, as well as for notes about meaning and pronunciation, etc.

Workbook Contents

Using the workbook

Most students find it easier to assimilate new vocabulary if the words are learned in related groups, rather than in isolation. For example, words frequently occur in the same context as their opposites and, as such, it makes sense to learn the pairs of opposites together (*see worksheets on pages 7 and 25*. Similarly, mind maps encourage students to look for connections between words (*see worksheet on page 9*). The exercises and activities in this workbook have all been grouped into sections. These sections practise different elements of marketing vocabulary, enabling the student to gain a fuller understanding of the words learnt.

The first section, **Word-building** (*pages 1-9*), encourages the student to identify links between words and to learn words that are morphologically related (for example, verbs and nouns which have the same stems). Within the **Parts of Speech** (*pages 10-17*) section, the emphasis is on understanding meanings and how to use terms in their correct grammatical forms. The worksheets in the third section practise the **Pronunciation** of marketing vocabulary (*pages 18-21*). The section **Vocabulary in Context** (*pages 22-32*) includes topic-specific exercises such as those on 'Telemarketing' and 'Designing sales literature'. The activities in the last section, **Puzzles & Quizzes** (*pages 33-36*), expand students' knowledge and use of vocabulary in a fun way.

Communicative crosswords

Included in the last section are four communicative crosswords. These are speaking exercises where students complete a half-finished crossword by exchanging clues with a partner. There are two versions of the crossword: A & B. The words which are missing from A are in B, and vice versa. No clues are provided: the students' task is to invent them. This is an excellent exercise for developing linguistic resourcefulness; in having to define words themselves, students practise both their marketing vocabulary and the important skill of paraphrasing something when they do not know the word for it.

Using Communicative crosswords

Stage 1 – Set-up. Divide the class into two groups - A and B - with up to four students in each group. Give out the crossword: sheet A to group A, sheet B to group B together with a copy of the *Dictionary of Marketing*. Go through the rules with them. Some answers may consist of more than one word.
Stage 2 - Preparation. The students discuss the words in their groups, exchanging information about the words they know and checking words they do not know in the **Dictionary of Marketing**. Circulate, helping with any problems. This is an important stage: some of the vocabulary in the crosswords is quite difficult.
Stage 3 - Activity. Put the students in pairs - one from group A and one from group B. The students help each other to complete the crosswords by giving each other clues.

Make sure students are aware that the idea is to help each other complete the crossword, rather than to produce obscure and difficult clues.

- What's one down?
- *It's a person who buys something.*
- A customer?
- *No, it's a customer who pays for a service.*
- A client?
- *Yes, that's right.*

A A	B B
A A	B B

Students work in groups, checking vocabulary

Alternatively, students can work in small groups, each group consisting of two As and two Bs and using the following strategies:
i)   defining the word
ii)   describing what the item looks like
iii)   stating what the item is used for
iv)   describing the person's role
v)   stating what the opposite of the word is
vi)   giving examples
vii)   leaving a gap in a sentence for the word
viii)   stating what the word sounds like.

A B	A B
A B	A B

Students work in pairs, co-operating to solve their crosswords

Word association 1: missing links

Each of the sets of four words below can be linked by one other word. All the words have business connections. What are the missing words? Write them in the centre of the charts.

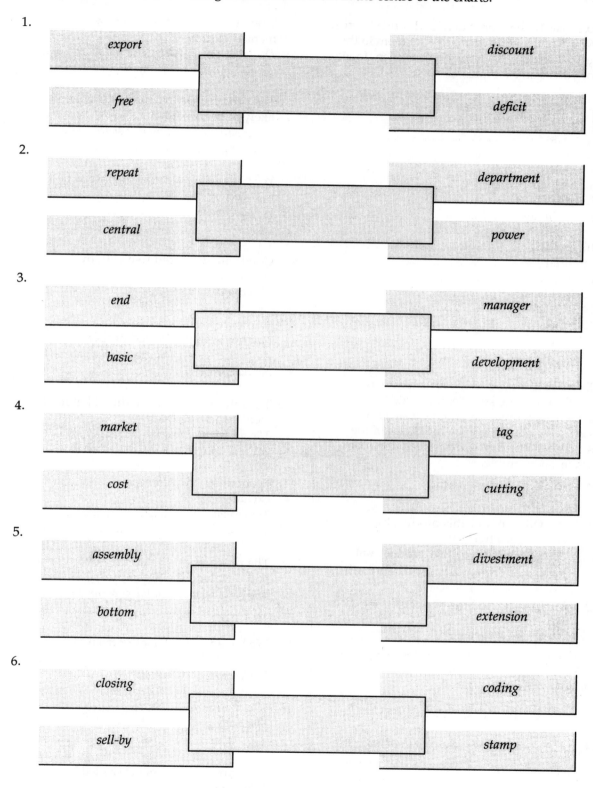

1.

| export | | discount |
| free | | deficit |

2.

| repeat | | department |
| central | | power |

3.

| end | | manager |
| basic | | development |

4.

| market | | tag |
| cost | | cutting |

5.

| assembly | | divestment |
| bottom | | extension |

6.

| closing | | coding |
| sell-by | | stamp |

Based on the **Dictionary of Marketing**
ISBN 0-948549-73-4
© Peter Collin Publishing

Word formation: nouns

A fast way to expand your vocabulary is to make sure you know the different forms of the words you learn.

Exercise 1. The words in this list are all verbs. What are the noun forms? Write them in the second column. The first one has been done for you as an example.

1. accept   .acceptance.......
2. agree   ....
3. classify   ....
4. decide   ....
5. delete   ....
6. deliver   ....
7. devaluate   ....
8. estimate   ....
9. forecast   ....
10. modify   ....
11. offer   ....
12. promote   ....
13. publicize   ....
14. select   ....
15. trade   ....

Exercise 2. First, check your answers to Exercise 1 in the key. Then rewrite the sentences below using nouns instead of verbs. Do not change the meanings of the sentences. The first one has been done for you as an example.

1. We will promote this product by offering customers a free gift.
   Our ..promotion of this product will involve offering customers a free gift...

2. We have agreed the budgets for next year.
   We have reached an ....
   ....

3. He estimated costs at £1m.
   His ....
   ....

4. The company trades with the US.
   The company does ....
   ....

5. They decided to appoint a new managing director.
   They took the ....
   ....

6. The product has lost market share and is likely to be deleted.
   The product has lost market share and is a likely candidate for ....

7. We have selected items that are to be reduced by 25%.
   We have made our ....
   ....

8. Goods are delivered free with this company.
   This company offers free ....

9. Audiences were small because the play had not been publicized properly.
   Audiences were small because the play had not had proper ....

10. The refrigerator was modified before it went into production.
    The refrigerator had ....
    ....

11. Economists have forecast a fall in the exchange rate.
    The economists' ....
    ....

12. The press reported that the government had devalued the dollar by 7%.
    The press reported on the government's ......
    ....

13. We have received a letter from him accepting the offer.
    We have received his letter of ....

14. She offered £10 a share.
    She made an ....
    ....

15. How are these papers classified?
    What's the ....
    ....

Based on the **Dictionary of Marketing**
ISBN 0-948549-73-4
© Peter Collin Publishing

Two-word expressions

Make 15 two-word expressions connected with business by combining words from the two lists: A and B. Match each expression with the appropriate phrase. Use each word once. The first one has been done for you as an example.

	A		B
A	assembly	**B**	break
	batch		card
	blind		income
	brand		interview
	colour		line
	commercial		list
	direct		~~mail~~
	directive		marketing
	disposable		number
	horse		power
	~~junk~~		supplement
	lead		testing
	mailing		time
	purchasing		trading
	rate		X

1. Unsolicited advertising material which is mailed and thrown away immediately by the people who receive it..**junk mail**...................

2. Production system in which the product (such as a car) moves slowly through the factory with new sections being added to it as it goes along
....

3. Number attached to a batch
....

4. Testing a product consumers without their knowing what brand it is
....

5. Magazine which accompanies a newspaper (usually with the weekend issue), printed in colour on art paper and containing a lot of advertising
....

6. Time set aside for commercials on television
....

7. Hard bargaining which ends with someone giving something in return for a concession from the other side
....

8. Income left after tax and national insurance have been deducted
....

9. Time between deciding to place an order and receiving the product
....

10. Selling a product direct to the customer without going through a shop
....

11. List of charges for advertising issued by a media owner (such as a magazine)
....

12. The anonymous brand which is used on TV commercials as a comparison to the named brand being advertised
....

13. List of names and addresses of people who might be interested in a product or list of names and addresses of members of a society
....

14. Quantity of goods which can be bought by a group of people or with a certain amount of money
....

15. Interview using preset questions and following a fixed pattern
....

Based on the **Dictionary of Marketing**
ISBN 0-948549-73-4
© Peter Collin Publishing

Plural formation

In *Column A* of this table there are 15 nouns relating to marketing. For each of the nouns decide whether the correct plural form is in *Column B* or *Column C* and then circle it. Be aware that in some instances the terms in *Column B* **and** *Column C* may both be correct plural forms and should therefore both be circled.

The first question has been done for you as an example.

	Column A	Column B	Column C
1.	emporium	(emporia)	emporiums
2.	trade fair	trades fair	trade fairs
3.	medium	mediums	media
4.	middleman	middlesman	middlemen
5.	branch	branches	branchs
6.	maximum	maximums	maxima
7.	curriculum vitae	curriculums vitae	curricula vitae
8.	sachet	sachets	sachetes
9.	consortium	consortia	consortiums
10.	adman	adsman	admen
11.	index	indexes	indices
12.	periodical	periodica	periodicals
13.	objective	objectives	objectiva
14.	saleswoman	saleswomans	saleswomen
15.	commercial agent	commercials agents	commercial agents

Based on the **Dictionary of Marketing**
ISBN 0-948549-73-4
© Peter Collin Publishing

Word formation: adjectives

The italicised words in the sentences in *Column A* are all nouns. What are the adjective forms? Complete the sentences in *Column B* using the correct adjective forms.

The first question has been done for you as an example.

	Column A	Column B
1.	He showed me evidence in the form of *documents*.	He showed me …documentary..evidence………………… …
2.	These goods can be taken in *exchange* for those items.	These goods are ……………………………………… ………………………………………
3.	There are variations in the sales patterns according to the *season*.	There are ……………………………………… ………………………………………
4.	The report mentioned the current *stability* of the currency markets.	The report mentioned that the currency markets are currently ……………………………………… ………………………………………
5.	She is a director of one of the *divisions*.	She is a ……………………………………… ………………………………………
6.	We have appointed a sales director who has a lot of *experience*.	We have appointed a very ……………………………………… ………………………………………
7.	The agencies operate within a framework of *self-regulation*.	The agencies operate within a ……………………………………… ………………………………………
8.	Development of the *economy* has been relatively slow in the north , compared with the rest of the country.	……………………………………… ………………………………………
9.	The economy has spiralling *inflation*.	The economy is in an ……………………………………… ………………………………………
10.	All sectors of *industry* have shown rises in output.	All ……………………………………… ………………………………………

Word association 2: partnerships

Exercise 1. Link each *verb* on the left with a *noun* on the right to make 10 'partnerships'. The first has been done for you as an example.

	VERBS	NOUNS
1.	manage	a payment
2.	lose	property
3.	freight	dues
4.	forfeit	an account
5.	exchange	a market
6.	effect	a target
7.	penetrate	contracts
8.	debit	customers
9.	release	a deposit
10.	meet	goods

Exercise 2. Complete these sentences using the partnerships from the first exercise. You may have to make some changes to fit the grammar of the sentences. The first one has been done for you as an example.

1. We should ...**meet**..... our ...**target**... of £2m for turnover this year.

2. They've been ....because their service is so slow.

3. They want to .... the US ....

4. We .... to all parts of the USA.

5. I shall get the accountant to .... the .... immediately.

6. The company .... in south-west London.

7. His .... was .... with the sum of £25.

8. I decided not to buy the item and .... my ....

9. We are due to .... this week, so should be in our new home shortly.

10. Now that the book is in stock, we can ....

Based on the **Dictionary of Marketing**
ISBN 0-948549-73-4
© Peter Collin Publishing Ltd

Opposites 1: prefixes

Exercise 1. Make the opposites of these words by adding prefixes: *im, in, ir* or *un*. The first one has been done for you as an example.

1. **un**..limited	6. .....stability
2. .....visible	7. .....controllable
3. .....direct	8. .....favourable
4. .....profitable	9. .....revocable
5. .....fair	10. .....load

Exercise 2. Complete these sentences using the opposites from Exercise 1. The first one has been done for you as an example.

1. Financial services and tourism are _____**invisible**_____ exports.

2. The sellers insisted on being paid by _____ letter of credit.

3. They need a fork-lift truck to _____ the lorry.

4. We are currently experiencing a period of _____ in the money markets.

5. It's _____ to expect them to do all the work.

6. The government obtains more revenue by _____ taxation than by direct.

7. The _____ exchange rate hit the country's exports.

8. This Internet account provides you with _____ e-mail addresses.

9. The international show was _____, and had to be subsidised by the government.

10. There are too many _____ variables for any real planning to take place.

Extension. Work with a partner and test each other. One partner closes the book, while the other asks questions such as *"What's the opposite of fair?"*.

Based on the **Dictionary of Marketing**
ISBN 0-948549-73-4
© Peter Collin Publishing Ltd

Word formation: verbs

Word-building

Exercise 1. The words listed in the table below are nouns. What are the verb forms of these nouns? The first question has been done for you as an example.

1.	acceptance .... *accept*	11.	integration
2.	adaptation	12.	launch
3.	adoption	13.	modification
4.	advertisement	14.	nullification
5.	agreement	15.	patronage
6.	approach	16.	permit
7.	confirmation	17.	selection
8.	decision	18.	subsidy
9.	discount	19.	trade
10.	installation	20.	turnover

Exercise 2. Choose ten verbs from Exercise 1 and write a sentence below for each one. Write the correct form of each verb in the column on the right and leave gaps for the verbs in the sentences. Cover up the right-hand column and give the sentences to another student as a test.

For example:

He ....£500 for the car.	*accepted*

1. ....

2. ....

3. ....

4. ....

5. ....

6. ....

7. ....

8. ....

9. ....

10. ....

Based on the **Dictionary of Marketing**
ISBN 0-948549-73-4
© Peter Collin Publishing Ltd

Word association 3: mind maps

A mind map is a way of organizing vocabulary to show the connections between words. This mind map is based on the word 'advertising'.

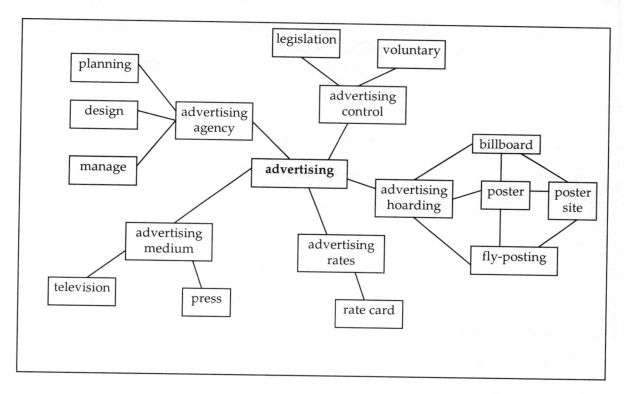

Exercise 1. Find words in the mind map which fit the following definitions.

1. Sticking posters up illegally, without permission of the site owner and without making any payment.
2. Newspapers and magazines.
3. Organizing how something should be done, especially how a company should be run to make increased profits.
4. Poster site of double crown size (30 x 20 inches).
5. Amount of money charged for advertising space in a newspaper or advertising time on TV.
6. Legislative and other measures to prevent abuses in advertising.
7. Laws.
8. Large eye-catching notice or advertisement which is stuck up outdoors or placed prominently inside a store.
9. Types of communication used in advertising such as television or the press.
10. List of charges for advertising issued by a media owner (such as a magazine).

Exercise 2. Design a mind map for one or more of the following:
* market
* price
* product.

Nouns

There are 18 words connected with marketing in the box below. Use them to complete the sentences. The first one has been done for you as an example.

brand	briefing	campaign	catalogue	chain	commission
enterprise	image	life-style	portfolio	presentation	~~prototype~~ quote
reach	researcher	shopping	trend	venue	

1. The company is showing the ____prototype____ of the new model at the exhibition.

2. We built the whole _____ round a well-known TV personality.

3. The _____ for the exhibition has been changed from the town hall to the conference

   centre.

4. They do all their _____ in the local supermarket.

5. Government statistics are a useful source of information for the desk _____ .

6. She bought several shoe shops and gradually built up a _____ .

7. The distribution company made a _____ of the services they could offer.

8. We notice a general _____ towards selling to the student market.

9. They are spending a lot of advertising money to improve the company's _____ .

10. All sales staff have to attend a sales _____ on the new product.

11. The company is launching a new _____ of soap.

12. These up-market products appeal to people with an extravagant _____ .

13. The project is completely funded by private _____ .

14. They sent us a _____ of their new range of desks.

15. The student brought a _____ of designs to show the design department manager.

16. The success of an advertisement depends on its _____ .

17. He gets 10% _____ on everything he sells.

18. They sent in their _____ for the job.

Based on the **Dictionary of Marketing**
ISBN 0-948549-73-4

Adjectives

Complete the sentences using the adjectives in the box. Use each adjective once only. The first one has been done for you as an example.

boxed	co-operative	cosmetic	exorbitant	extensive	false	fragile
frequent	~~immediate~~	imperfect	inferior	limiting	nationwide	normal
reciprocal	refundable	seasonal	socio-economic

1. He wrote an _____**immediate**_____ letter of complaint.

2. We've made some _____ changes to our product line.

3. The demand for this item is very _____ .

4. We send _____ faxes to New York.

5. The books are sold as a _____ set.

6. He made a _____ entry in the balance sheet.

7. The short holiday season is a _____ factor on the hotel trade.

8. Now that the strike is over we hope to resume _____ service as soon as possible.

9. They signed a _____ trade agreement.

10. We offer a _____ delivery service.

11. We have commissioned a thorough _____ analysis of our potential market.

12. Their fees may seem _____ , but their costs are very high.

13. There is an extra premium for insuring _____ goods in shipment.

14. Margarine was clearly an _____ product before it came to be considered healthier than butter.

15. We checked the batch for _____ products.

16. The workforce have not been _____ over the management's productivity plan.

17. The entrance fee is _____ if you purchase £5 worth of goods.

18. The company has an _____ network of sales outlets.

Based on the **Dictionary of Marketing**
ISBN 0-948549-73-4
© Peter Collin Publishing Ltd

Verbs

All the verbs in the box relate to marketing. Use them to complete the sentences. The first question has been done for you as an example.

---

advertise   brief   budget   buy   distribute

~~guarantee~~   insert   price   relaunch   report   research   sample   select

sponsor   target

---

1. The manufacturer will ___guarantee___ the product for twelve months.

2. The sales department is likely to _____ an increased demand for the product.

3. He is going to _____ the car at £5,000.

4. The managing director will _____ the board on the progress of the negotiations.

5. Many people in PR are using direct marketing as a precise means to _____ the market.

6. We will _____ for £10,000 of sales next year.

7. The research department has been asked to _____ the packaging of the new product line.

8. They will _____ profits among the shareholders.

9. As part of their new marketing strategy, the company decided to _____ a television programme.

10. She will _____ which items are to be reduced by 25%.

11. The marketing department has decided to _____ a publicity piece in this month's magazine mailing.

12. Smith Ltd will _____ the product with some minor modifications next autumn.

13. They _____ wholesale and sell retail.

14. The company is going to _____ the vacancy.

15. Our brief is to _____ 2,000 people at random to test the new drink.

Based on the **Dictionary of Marketing**
ISBN 0-948549-73-4
© Peter Collin Publishing Ltd

Verbs: past tense ~ regular verbs

All the verbs in the box relate to marketing. Use the past tense forms to complete the sentences.

The first question has been done for you as an example.

```
access    adopt    analyze    display    express    handle    pack
        pioneer    post    set    shift    transport
```

1. They __shifted__ 20,000 items in one week.

2. She _____ the address file on the computer.

3. We _____ the price of the computer low, so as to achieve the maximum unit sales.

4. We _____ the market potential of the newly designed computer table.

5. Previously a public relations firm _____ all our publicity, but now it is all done in-house.

6. We _____ the order to the customer's warehouse.

7. I _____ the goods into cartons before shipping them.

8. The company _____ three new car models at the show.

9. They _____ the visitors by helicopter to their factory.

10. The company _____ developments in the field of electronics.

11. Last month we _____ a new marketing strategy.

12. She _____ the leaflets yesterday.

Verbs: mixed tenses

All the verbs in the box relate to marketing matters. Use them to complete the sentences. You may have to change the forms of the verbs to fit the grammar of the sentences. (Remember the five forms of English verbs - for example: take, takes, took, taken, taking.)

The first question has been done for you as an example.

approve	compete	expand	maximize	outbid
outsell	promote	~~reach~~	record	switch
	tip	undersell		

1. What percentage of the target audience did the advertisement ____**reach**____?

2. The company has _____ another year of increased sales.

3. We must consider ways of _____ the new product.

4. The proposal was _____ by the board.

5. Management's aim is to _____ profits.

6. Companies often _____ from undifferentiated to differentiated marketing during a product's life cycle.

7. This company is never _____ .

8. He is _____ to become the next marketing manager.

9. We offered £100,000 for the warehouse, but another company _____ us.

10. The two companies are _____ for a market share.

11. They have had to _____ their sales force.

12. The company is easily _____ its competitors.

Based on the **Dictionary of Marketing**
ISBN 0-948549-73-4
© Peter Collin Publishing Ltd

Phrasal verbs

Natural English conversation includes many phrasal verbs. These are verbs made up of two words: a verb and a preposition. For example: 'I *get up* at eight o'clock'. Complete the sentences below with the phrasal verbs in the box. You will have to change the forms of some of the verbs to make the grammar of the sentence correct. The first one has been done for you as an example.

1. The new managing director ____**hived off** the retail sections of the company.

2. We are _____ _____ a pocket calculator with each £10 of purchases.

3. From car retailing, the company _____ _____ into car leasing.

4. The company was _____ _____ and separate divisions sold off.

5. The reps have to _____ _____ all their expenses to the sales manager.

6. These prices have been _____ _____ by 10%.

7. We _____ _____ money on that house.

8. The company is letting stocks _____ _____.

9. The bill is _____ _____ to Smith & Co.

10. We _____ _____ an outside agency to handle all our promotion.

11. The government is _____ _____ an inquiry.

12. At 6pm the cashiers _____ _____.

Verbs
i.   *account for* = to explain and record a money deal
ii.   *branch out* = to start a new (but usually related) type of business
iii. *break up* = to split something large into small sections
iv.   *call in* = to ask someone for help
v.   *cash up* = to add up the cash in a shop at the end of a day
vi.   *give away* = to give something as a free present
vii. *hive off* = to split off part of a large company to form a smaller subsidiary
viii. *make out* = to write
ix.   *mark up* = to increase the price of something
x.   *put down* = to make a deposit
xi.   *run down* = to reduce a quantity gradually
xii. *set up* = to begin (something) or to organize (something)

Extension. Work with a partner: write a dialogue which includes at least seven of the phrasal verbs on this page.

Based on the **Dictionary of Marketing**
ISBN 0-948549-73-4
© Peter Collin Publishing Ltd

Adverbs

The sentences below do not read correctly. Identify the adverbs in the sentences and then swap the adverbs around so that each sentence makes sense.

Some of the adverbs could be used in several of the sentences, but in order to complete the exercise successfully, all the sentences must make sense.

1. The project is not voluntarily viable.

    ....

2. The contract is privately binding.

    ....

3. The company is competitively sound.

    ....

4. The computer internally forecast that sales would drop in the second quarter.

    ....

5. He updated the database commercially.

    ....

6. The deal was negotiated frequently.

    ....

7. Their products are legally priced.

    ....

8. The photocopier is financially out of order.

    ....

9. The job was advertised directly.

    ....

10. We deal accurately with the manufacturer, without using a wholesaler.

    ....

Based on the **Dictionary of Marketing**
ISBN 0-948549-73-4
© Peter Collin Publishing Ltd

Prepositions

The sentences in this exercise contain **mistakes**. The mistakes are all in the prepositions and there are three types:

1.	missing preposition	I spoke ^him about this last week. *to*
2.	wrong preposition	We're meeting again ~~in~~ ^Tuesday. *on*
3.	unnecessary preposition	I'll telephone ~~to~~ you tomorrow.

Find the mistakes and correct them.

1. We have a file of press cuttings over our rivals' products.

2. Both consumer markets and industrial markets have been affected through the recession.

3. The company will start work the project next month.

4. We are short by staff.

5. Profits were distributed at the shareholders.

6. These prices have been marked up 10%.

7. He received confirmation the bank that the deeds had been deposited.

8. We offer to a nationwide delivery service.

9. We plan to build a factory to the Far East.

10. The marketing director's brief was to increase coverage through at least 10%.

11. The company spends at thousands of pounds on research.

12. Consumers are found to be especially influenced by the tastes and opinions of those per their peer groups.

13. They have agreed the budgets over next year.

14. Please send me literature to your new product range.

Based on the **Dictionary of Marketing**
ISBN 0-948549-73-4
© Peter Collin Publishing Ltd

Word stress

One of the keys to English pronunciation is *stress* - emphasis. There are three possible patterns for three-syllable words:

A: ■□□   **hol**-i-day
B: □■□   pro-**duc**-tion
C: □□■   em-ploy-**ee**

Read these three conversations. Find all the three-syllable words and classify them by their pronunciation. There are 13 in total. Put them in the correct sections of the table on the right. The first one has been done for you as an example.

Dialogue 1
°   What are your thoughts on this product?
•   Well, firstly we shall have to obtain the <u>patentee</u>'s permission to manufacture it. Then I think the packaging needs to be more original to improve brand recognition. Also, I think it should be sold with a 12-month guarantee.
°   I agree with you. And our market research certainly bears out your packaging comment, so I think we'd better refer it back to the design department.
•   Good idea.

Dialogue 2
°   What marketing strategy do you suggest that we adopt to reach these long-term objectives?
•   I think we should expand through product diversification and market development.
°   So we'd be looking to add new types of products to our range, while at the same time searching for and exploiting new markets for our core products.
•   Yes, that's it.

Dialogue 3
°   As a sales rep for this company, what do you see your main tasks to be?
•   Prospecting for new customers, giving them information about our products, selling the products, and market research.
°   And how do you relate the 'marketing concept' to your role within the company?
•   I am less concerned with generating short-term sales, and more with keeping customers satisfied, bringing back market information, gaining long-term sales and hence maximising profits.

Group A: ■□□
Group B: □■□
Group C: □□■
patentee

Extension. Practise the dialogues with a partner.

Based on the **Dictionary of Marketing**
ISBN 0-948549-73-4
© Peter Collin Publishing Ltd

Verbs & nouns

Sometimes two words can be spelled the same but pronounced differently. This is often because one word is a noun and the other is a verb. One example is the word `import':

1. Oil is a major **im**-port for France.   NOUN ❶② stress on the first syllable
2. Does Britain im-**port** a lot of wine?   VERB ①❷ stress on the second syllable

Read the following sentences. Decide in each case if the word in *italics* is a verb or a noun. Then decide which stress pattern it has and complete the table. The first one has been done for you as an example.

		noun/ verb	❶②	①❷
1.	France, Spain, Greece and Italy *export* olive oil.	verb		x
2.	Manufactured goods are Japan's principal *export*.			
3.	The visitors will be using public *transport*.			
4.	The company will *transport* the visitors to the factory by helicopter.			
5.	She is going to *permit* us to use her name in the advertising copy.			
6.	Do you have an export *permit*?			
7.	The company will *indent* for a new computer.			
8.	He put in an *indent* for a new stock of soap.			
9.	They will *subcontract* the electrical work to Smith Ltd.			
10.	They have been awarded the *subcontract* for all the electrical work in the new building.			
11.	They have farm *produce* for sale.			
12.	Both companies *produce* engines.			
13.	The company will *record* another year of increased sales.			
14.	Our top salesperson has set a new *record* of sales per call.			

Based on the **Dictionary of Marketing**
ISBN 0-948549-73-4
© Peter Collin Publishing Ltd

Present simple

Verbs in the present tense add an 's' in the third person singular: I work, you work, he/she/it works. But the 's' has three different pronunciations. Look at these examples:

A: /s/, for example *markets*
B: /z/, for example *sells*
C: /Iz/, for example *closes*

Find the third person present tense verbs in these sentences and classify them by their pronunciation. Put them in the correct columns in the table on the right. Be careful: some sentences have more than one example. There are 21 examples in total. The first one has been done for you as an example.

Group A: /s/
1. **inserts**
2..
3.
4.
5.
6.
7.
8.

Group B: /z/
1.
2.
3.
4.
5.

Group C: /Iz/
1.
2.
3.
4.
5.
6.
7.
8.

1. He <u>inserts</u> a publicity piece in the magazine each month.

2. The warehouseman dispatches the goods every Thursday.

3. The agent always faxes us details of new product launches.

4. He advises us on design issues.

5. The shop takes £2,000 a week.

6. She buys wholesale for her retail outlet.

7. The R&D department researches and tests new products.

8. I think it's an excellent plan, and our marketing director agrees.

9. She manages the department.

10. Supply and demand regulates prices.

11. The company charges packing to the customer.

12. He collects the stock from the warehouse every Monday morning.

13. The sales manager reports direct to the managing director.

14. Each of these companies delivers goods free.

15. He deals in leather goods.

16. This soft drinks company advertises heavily.

17. She packs the goods into cartons.

18. The public holiday falls on a Tuesday.

19. Our company produces and markets computers.

Extension. The same rule applies to plural nouns: /s/ cost<u>s</u>, /z/ sale<u>s</u>, /Iz/ expense<u>s</u>. Work with a partner and find five example nouns for each sound.

Based on the **Dictionary of Marketing**
ISBN 0-948549-73-4
© Peter Collin Publishing Ltd

Past simple

Regular verbs have three different pronunciations in the past tense (or the past participle). The difference is in the sound you use for the ending. Look at these examples:

A: /t/, for example work*ed*
B: /d/, for example clos*ed*
C: /Id/, for example start*ed*

Find the past tense verbs in these sentences and classify them by their pronunciation. Put them in the correct columns in the table on the right. The first one has been done for you as an example.

1. They ~~launched~~ their new car model at the motor show.

2. We shipped the consignment of cars abroad last week.

3. The company traded under the name 'Eeziphitt'.

4. We publicized our products by using advertisements on buses.

5. The salesmen called on their best accounts twice last month.

6. She recently opened a shop in the High Street.

7. The agent faxed us details of the product launch.

8. The managing director organized the company into six profit areas.

9. In the past, the company always exported the finished products.

10. The sales manager budgeted for £10,000 of sales this year.

11. He charged £5 for delivery.

12. We financed the operation with borrowed money.

13. They mailed their catalogue to 3,000 customers in Europe.

14. We marketed this in all European countries.

Group A: /t/	
1	launched
2	
3	
4	
Group B: /d/	
1	
2	
3	
4	
5	
6	
Group C: /Id/	
1	
2	
3	
4	

Based on the **Dictionary of Marketing**
ISBN 0-948549-73-4
© Peter Collin Publishing Ltd

Marketing metaphors

A metaphor is a way of describing something by giving it the qualities of something else. Many of the verbs and nouns used in marketing are metaphors. For example: a product range can be *pruned* — like a tree — meaning that the range can be reduced by removing old products.

Link the words in the box with their literal meanings below. Then define each word in a marketing context. The first question has been done for you as an example.

battle	blitz	~~campaign~~	capture	flood	launch
	saturate	tactic	target	territory	

1. organized military attack
......*campaign:* series of co-ordinated activities to reach an objective..........................

2. to cover with water
....

3. object which you aim at with a gun, etc.
....

4. important fight between armed forces
....

5. to take someone or something as a prisoner
....

6. to fill something with the maximum amount of a liquid or a substance that can be absorbed
....

7. land which belongs to a country
....

8. bombing by planes
....

9. to put a boat into the water, especially for the first time and with a lot of ceremony
....

10. way of fighting a war
....

Extension. With a partner, write sentences using each of the words in the list in a marketing context.

Based on the **Dictionary of Marketing**
ISBN 0-948549-73-4
© Peter Collin Publishing Ltd

Categories: the four P's

In this table there are 24 aspects of marketing and four categories of the marketing mix — Product, Price, Promotion and Place. Decide which category each aspect of marketing belongs to. The first one has been done for you as an example.

	Product	Price	Promotion	Place
line extension	x			
warehousing				
brand name				
commercials				
competitive pricing				
point of purchase				
transportation				
price list				
guarantee				
packaging				
quality control				
manufacturing costs				
free sample				
retail outlet				
product design				
mailshot				
advertising				
quantity discount				
sponsor				
payment on delivery				
distribution channels				
publicity campaign				
credit account				
inventory				

Based on the **Dictionary of Marketing**
ISBN 0-948549-73-4
© Peter Collin Publishing Ltd

Odd one out

In each set of words one is the *odd one out*: different from the others. Find the word or phrase that is different, and circle it. For example:

> (aeroplane) .... *fax* .... *phone* .... *telex*

'Aeroplane' is the odd one out. The others are all used to communicate information.

1. red goods .... yellow goods .... FMCGs .... convenience goods

2. patterned .... directive .... depth .... structured

3. marketing manager .... customer .... designer .... sales representative

4. survivors .... achievers .... emulators .... consumers

5. acquire .... buy .... purchase .... sell

6. costly .... dear .... economical .... expensive

7. ask for .... demand .... offer .... request

8. abroad .... domestic .... foreign .... overseas

9. cold call .... hotline .... sales representative ..... sales call

10. turnover .... sales revenue .... takings .... by-product

11. tannoy .... advertising hoarding .... poster .... billboard

12. monthly .... quarterly .... weekly .... frequently

13. home .... domestic .... international .... internal

14. closing date .... use-by date .... sell-by date .... best-before date

Based on the **Dictionary of Marketing**
ISBN 0-948549-73-4
© Peter Collin Publishing Ltd

Opposites 2

Exercise 1. Match the words in *italics* with their opposites in the box on the right. The first one has been done for you as an example.

1. The opposite of *sell* is .... **buy** ....
2. The opposite of *profit* is..
3. The opposite of *vertical* is ....
4. The opposite of *negative* is ....
5. The opposite of *win* is ....
6. The opposite of *late* is...
7. The opposite of *downturn* is ....
8. The opposite of *up market* is ....
9. The opposite of *heterogeneous* is..
10. The opposite of *boom* is..

> early
> recession
> loss
> lose
> homogeneous
> down market
> ~~buy~~
> horizontal
> positive
> upturn

Exercise 2. Complete these sentences using the words from Exercise 1. Use one word from each pair of opposites.

1. They tried to_____**sell**_____ their house for £200,000.

2. A _____ industrial market is a market in which a product is used by many industries.

3. The managing director is pleased because costs this year show a £60,000 _____ variance.

4. The company is breaking even now and expects to move into _____ within the next two months.

5. There is a penalty for _____ delivery.

6. We are pleased to report that there has been an _____ in the economy.

7. These are _____ shopping goods, in that they vary little in style and quality from brand to brand and consumers spend little time choosing them.

8. Our offices are _____ from 9am to 5pm.

9. Several firms have closed factories because of the _____ .

10. The directors are pleased that their company looks set to _____ a contract worth £25m.

Extension. Work with a partner and test each other. One partner closes the book, while the other asks questions such as *"What's the opposite of open?"*.

Abbreviations

Test your marketing abbreviations. What do the following stand for? Check the ones you don't know in the dictionary. The first one has been done for you as an example.

1. VAT   *Value Added Tax* ....

2. NPD   ....

3. GHI   ....

4. USP   ....

5. EPOS ....

6. PR   ....

7. L/C   ....

8. ad   ....

9. R&D   ....

10. KD   ....

11. MRP   ....

12. DM   ....

13. o.n.o. ....

14. acct   ....

15. RRP   ....

16. POS   ....

17. OFT   ....

18. POPA   ....

19. c.o.d. ....

20. JIT   ....

21. FMCGs ....

22. OTS   ....

Extension. Work with a partner and test each other. One partner closes the book, the other asks questions. For example: *"What does VAT stand for?"*

Based on the **Dictionary of Marketing**
ISBN 0-948549-73-4
© Peter Collin Publishing Ltd

Flow charts

A flow chart is a diagram that shows the sequence of steps in a procedure or production process. Place the steps in each of the marketing flow charts below in the correct sequence.

1. Advertising

advertising campaign >>> advertising brief >>> advertisement >>> media planning

.... >>> .... >>> .... >>> ....

2. Consumer response

desire >>> action >>> attention >>> interest

.... >>> .... >>> .... >>> ....

3. Distribution

consumer >>> manufacturer >>> retailer >>> wholesaler

.... >>> .... >>> .... >>> ....

4. Product

distribution >>> manufacture >>> selling >>> launch >>> design >>>

concept >>> testing >>> development >>> idea testing

.... >>> .... >>> .... >>> .... >>> .... >>>

.... >>> .... >>> .... >>> ....

5. Product life cycle

maturity >>> launch >>> decline >>> growth

.... >>> .... >>> .... >>> ....

Extension. Work with a partner and write a paragraph for one of the above sequences, using all the terms from the flow chart.

Telemarketing

Telemarketing involves marketing a product or service over the telephone. Complete the examples of telemarketing usage using the words in the box below.

---

calls	canvass	concept	customer	handle	incentives
mailshot	products	sales	sectors	targeted	update

Market research
Telemarketing can be used for:

- (1) .... testing

- testing (2) .... reaction to new (3) ....

- identifying new market (4) ....

- finding out who should be (5) .... with sales information within organisations

- testing prices/offers/(6) ....

As part of a direct marketing campaign
Telemarketing is an effective way to:

- (7) .... mailing lists

- canvass (8) .... leads

- follow up a (9) ....

Generating sales opportunities for sales representatives
Telemarketing is a good way to:

- (10) .... sales leads

- arrange sales (11) ....

Building customer relations
Telemarketing can be used to:

- (12) .... customer complaints and enquiries.

Extension. Work with a partner. Choose a product and work out a framework for calls that a telesales person could use as part of a telemarketing campaign for that product. Remember the framework should be a basis for questions rather than a script to be read. Think about the product being marketed, the selling benefits that are relevant to the market being contacted, whether an offer would be appropriate, how the customer can pay and what further information is available if the prospect asks for more details.

Based on the **Dictionary of Marketing**
ISBN 0-948549-73-4
© Peter Collin Publishing Ltd

Promotional tools

Promotional material can take a variety of different formats. The list below is a selection of these formats. Define each one.

1. Catalogues

    ....

2. Leaflets and fliers

    ....

3. Posters

    ....

4. Advertorials

    ....

5. Radio ads

    ....

6. Television ads

    ....

7. Classified ads

    ....

8. Semi-display ads

    ....

Extension. Working with a partner, write a 30-second radio advertisement for a product of your choice. Remember that during a radio commercial the product name is often continually repeated to get it across to the audience.

Based on the **Dictionary of Marketing**
ISBN 0-948549-73-4
© Peter Collin Publishing Ltd

Agency awards

Agencies often compete on an annual basis for awards which recognise excellence within the field of marketing.

Below is a list of fictitious awards, together with details on these awards. Match the award titles in Column A with the correct details in Column B.

Column A	Column B
1. **Best use of advertising**	a) Awarded to the best promotional marketing campaign using direct marketing as the main promotional format. The judges are looking for evidence of successful targeting to achieve set objectives.
2. **Best use of new media**	b) Awarded to the best promotional marketing campaign that has run in more than one international market.
3. **Best business to business campaign**	c) Awarded to the promotional marketing campaign with the best creative use of trade or consumer advertising media. The judges are looking for the message to be clear, with high quality delivery and strong calls for action to secure the product.
4. **Best use of direct marketing**	d) Awarded to the best promotional marketing campaign that specifically targets business customers.
5. **Best international campaign**	e) Awarded to the promotional marketing campaign that uses digital/electronic or other interactive media as a main element of the communication to best effect.

Extension. Choose one of the above fictitious awards and, imagining that you are a director of an agency, summarise a promotional marketing campaign developed by your agency, explaining how your entry qualifies for the award.

Based on the **Dictionary of Marketing**
ISBN 0-948549-73-4
© Peter Collin Publishing Ltd

Designing sales literature

Sales literature is any printed information (such as leaflets and prospectuses) which helps sales. A well-designed piece of sales literature will encourage the relevant market to read it, absorb the sales message and act on the recommendation to buy.

An important element in the preparation of sales literature is therefore design. Once copy for sales literature has been written and checked, the layout needs to be planned. The following are some tips for designing sales literature. Select the correct alternatives to complete the text. The first question has been done for you as an example.

- Make sure that it is easy for the reader to home in on the benefits of the (1) **(b)** ...**product**... being advertised.

- Make any headings and subheadings clear. Don't use upper case letters too much – they are hard to read and prevent words from being (2) .... at a glance.

- Ensure that the sales (3) .... is visually varied without being too fussy. Use bullet points, vary paragraph length and don't have text justified. Illustrations provide a welcome break from text.

- Put a box around particularly important text or highlight it by using a different typeface or colour. However, remember that any typeface or colour used must be legible; excessive use of italics and bright colours makes text difficult to read.

- Avoid over-filling the (4) .... A (5) .... that looks confused or is difficult to read will put the reader off. Space attracts (6) .... so allow plenty to get the reader involved.

- Don't put extensive amounts of copy at an angle; it is very difficult to read. An exception is a flash across the corner of an (7) .... – this can be a very effective way of attracting attention.

- Position an advertisement on a right-hand page in preference to a left-hand page. An advertisement that faces text rather than another advertisement is also preferable - most readers flick past (8) .... of advertising.

- The (9) .... in a direct (10) .... advertisement should be placed where it is easiest to cut out.

1.a) productive	b) product	c) productivity
2.a) reciprocated	b) recognized	c) regulated
3.a) literature	b) lineage	c)` ledger
4.a) space	b) specimen	c) specification
5.a) format	b) form utility	c) forecast
6.a) audit	b) attrition	c) attention
7.a) adspend	b) advertising	c) advert
8.a) single column centimetres	b) double page spreads	c) deep-rooted demand
9.a) coupon	b) counter-offer	c) coverage
10.a) respondent	b) resale	c) response

Extension. To increase your awareness of design in a marketing context, scan printed media for advertisements and assess their impact by discussing them with a partner.

Based on the **Dictionary of Marketing**
ISBN 0-948549-73-4
© Peter Collin Publishing Ltd

Talking about marketing

The Marketing Manager and the Managing Director of XYZoft, a computer company, are discussing the marketing of a new program. Find the words in the conversation which fit the definitions in the box. The first one has been done for you as an example.

○ How are you going to promote Construct-X?

● *Well, first of all we'll include it in the new catalogue.*

○ OK. What about advertising?

● *We're going to run a campaign in the press, but only in specialist publications. This is a niche product.*

○ Right. Are you going to do a mailing?

● *Yes, just a flier to our regular customers.*

○ Will you offer them any kind of giveaway?

● *No, but there will be a discount on orders in the first thirty days.*

○ Sounds good.

● *Well, we'll see.*

○ Do you think we should focus mainly on the domestic market or go for overseas sales right at the beginning?

● *I think domestic to start with. That way we don't have to worry about distribution problems until later.*

○ I think I agree. What about pricing?

● *Well, this is a unique product, there's no real competition, so it's going to be fairly high-priced. Don't you think so?*

○ Well, that sounds fair. Any thoughts about the package?

● *Standard - a hard case containing the discs and the manual. Technical drawings on the outside to give a precise, professional image.*

○ Are you going to have any <u>point-of-sale</u> displays in computer shops?

● *Just a poster, using the same image as the packaging.*

○ Well, it all sounds very good.

● *You'll find all the details in this report.*

1. a place where a product is sold
   point-of-sale ....

2. series of co-ordinated activities to reach an objective
   ....

3. giving a price to a product
   ....

4. person or company which buys goods
   ....

5. market in the country where a company is based
   ....

6. promotional leaflet
   ....

7. thing which is given as a free gift when another item is bought
   ....

8. general idea that the public has of a product, brand or company
   ....

9. sending in the post
   ....

10. special place in a market, occupied by one company
    ....

11. attractive material used to wrap goods for display
    ....

12. publication which lists items for sale, usually showing their prices
    ....

13. percentage by which the seller reduces the full price for the buyer
    ....

14. to advertise
    ....

15. business of announcing that something is for sale or of trying to persuade customers to buy a product or service
    ....

16. act of sending goods from the manufacturer to the wholesaler and then to the retailers
    ....

17. trying to do better than another supplier or to win over some of its customers
    ....

18. foreign countries
    ....

Extension. Practise the conversation with a partner.

Based on the **Dictionary of Marketing**
ISBN 0-948549-73-4
© Peter Collin Publishing Ltd

Anagrams 1

Solve the anagrams by reading the clues and putting the letters in order to form words. Write your answers in the grid to find the mystery word spelled by their initial letters. The first one has been done for you as an example.

1. Situation where one person or company is the only supplier of a particular
    product or service...MLOMOPYNO

2. Show of goods so that buyers can look at them and decide what to buy...........THIXIBIONE

3. Act of sponsoring...ROSSPINSOPH

4. Plan of future action...STYGREAT

5. Detailed examination and report...YILANASS

6. Showing a little of the product itself by removing a small part of the
    packaging..GINGTOSH

7. Publicity given to an organization or product...PEXURESO

1	M	O	N	O	P	O	L	Y		
2										
3										
4									
5									
6									
7									

Mystery Word Clue: idea that is communicated by promotion

Based on the **Dictionary of Marketing**
ISBN 0-948549-73-4
© Peter Collin Publishing Ltd

Communicative crossword 1   sheet A

This crossword is not complete: you have only half the words. The other half are on sheet B. Check that you know the words in your crossword. Then work with a partner who has sheet B to complete the two crosswords. Follow these three rules:

1	Speak only in English.
2	Don't say the word in the crossword.
3	Don't show your partner the crossword.

> `What's 1 across?'
>
> → **Across,** ↓ **Down**

Based on the **Dictionary of Marketing**
ISBN 0-948549-73-4
© Peter Collin Publishing Ltd

Communicative crossword 1   sheet B

This crossword is not complete: you have only half the words. The other half are on sheet A. Check that you know the words in your crossword. Then work with a partner who has sheet A to complete the two crosswords. Follow these three rules:

1. Speak only in English.

2. Don't say the word in the crossword.

3. Don't show your partner the crossword.

> `What's 1 across?'
>
> → **Across,** ↓ **Down**

Based on the **Dictionary of Marketing**
ISBN 0-948549-73-4
© Peter Collin Publishing Ltd

Word search

Find the 24 marketing terms and expressions hidden in the letters below; 12 read across and 12 read down. One word has been found for you as an example. The clues listed beneath should help you to find all the words.

A	G	C̶	O̶	P̶	Y̶	W̶	R̶	I̶	T̶	E̶	R̶
F	E	E	D	B	C	E	D	E	E	N	E
F	N	M	I	S	S	I	O	N	L	C	P
M	E	D	I	A	T	G	S	G	E	L	O
A	R	A	C	K	R	H	P	C	M	O	S
R	I	V	A	L	A	T	H	O	A	S	I
T	C	H	I	P	T	I	E	P	R	U	T
S	A	M	P	L	E	N	R	Y	K	R	I
O	F	F	E	O	G	G	E	J	E	E	O
L	K	L	G	Y	Y	D	E	P	T	H	N
U	F	A	I	R	M	O	U	T	E	R	N
S	P	I	N	O	F	F	O	P	R	Q	R

1. _____ date = date by which an advertisement must be delivered to the media concerned
2. Person who writes copy for advertisements
3. Variety in a product line
4. Document enclosed with a letter or package
5. trade _____ = large exhibition and meeting for advertising and selling a certain type of product
6. To give information or tips to another salesman, regarding promising customers or areas for sales
7. Product sold without a brand name
8. Market, a place where things are sold
9. Means of communicating a message (about a product or service) to the audience
10. The long-term objectives of an organization
11. Subtracted from
12. Packaging which covers items that are already in packages
13. Off-the-_____ clothes = clothes which are made ready to wear in certain standard sizes
14. Trick or gimmick, used to attract customers
15. Frame to hold items for display
16. To change the position of a product or company in the market
17. Person or company which competes in the same market
18. Specimen, a small part of an item which is used to show what the whole item is like
19. _____ advertisement = advertisement which does not appear near other advertisements for similar products
20. Area
21. Useful product developed as a secondary product from a main item
22. Plan of future action
23. Person who markets a product by telephone
24. Statistical process which gives more importance to some figures than others in the process of reaching a final figure or result

Based on the **Dictionary of Marketing**
ISBN 0-948549-73-4
© Peter Collin Publishing Ltd

Marketing crossword 1

All the answers in this crossword are connected with marketing.

Across
1. Something which you hope to achieve
5. Subtracted from
7. Attracting the attention of the public to products or services by mentioning them in the media
8. Arrangement of different things together; e.g. marketing _____.
10. Abbreviation for 'representative'
12. With everything added together
13. Abbreviation for 'operational research'
15. Statement that you are willing to pay a certain amount of money to buy something
17. General rule
18. Abbreviation for 'information technology'
19. Excessive claims made in advertising
20. Possible harm or chance of danger

Down
1. Chance to do something successfully
2. Piece of work or order being worked on
3. Person who pays for a service
4. Thing which is a copy of an original
6. Facsimile copy, sent via the telephone lines
9. To bring goods from abroad into a country for sale
11. Description of the characteristics of something
16. Promotional leaflet

Based on the **Dictionary of Marketing**
ISBN 0-948549-73-4
© Peter Collin Publishing Ltd

Communicative crossword 2   sheet A

This crossword is not complete: you have only half the words. The other half are on sheet B. Check that you know the words in your crossword. Then work with a partner who has sheet B to complete the two crosswords. Follow these three rules:

1	Speak only in English.
2	Don't say the word in the crossword.
3	Don't show your partner the crossword.

> `What's 1 across?'
>
> → **Across,** ↓ **Down**

The crossword grid contains the following filled letters:

- 1 across: CAMPAIGN (with ¹C A M ²P A ³I G N)
- ⁴S at top right
- Row 2: ⁵T, L
- 6 across: ⁶N O T E, ⁷S ..., E, O
- Row: T, S, T
- 8 across: ⁸E L ⁹A S T I C I T ¹⁰Y
- 11
- Row: N, T
- 12 across: ¹²T E A M
- L, U, 13
- 14, Y, ¹⁵F I X
- S, O, ¹⁶S H O P
- 17, E, N
- ¹⁸T O K E N

Based on the **Dictionary of Marketing**
ISBN 0-948549-73-4
© Peter Collin Publishing Ltd

Communicative crossword 2   sheet B

This crossword is not complete: you have only half the words. The other half are on sheet A. Check that you know the words in your crossword. Then work with a partner who has sheet A to complete the two crosswords. Follow these three rules:

1   Speak only in English.

2   Don't say the word in the crossword.

3   Don't show your partner the crossword.

`What's 1 across?'

→ **Across,** ↓ **Down**

Anagrams 2

Solve the anagrams by reading the clues and putting the letters in order to form words. Write your answers in the grid to find the mystery word spelled by their initial letters. The first one has been done for you as an example.

1. Poster of double crown size .... CLADARP

2. Person who carries out research .... CHREARESER

3. Increase in size .... NOISPENAX

4. Detailed report on a problem or particular subject .... RYSEUV

5. To examine something to see how good it is .... LEAVUTEA

6. Reaching only a small, special audience through an electronic medium such as

   cable television .... GROWNSTRAINCA

7. List of figures or facts set out in columns .... LETBA

8. Decrease in the loyalty of consumers to a product, due to boredom, desire for a

   change, etc. .... INOTATRIT

9. Label .... AGT

10. To bring in new ideas or new methods .... NETONAVI

11. Where something comes from .... IRINOG

12. Word used to call a thing or a person by .... MEAN

1	P	L	A	C	A	R	D				
2											
3											
4											
5											
6											
7											
8											
9											
10											
11											
12											

Mystery Word Clue: demonstration or exhibition of a proposed plan

Based on the **Dictionary of Marketing**
ISBN 0-948549-73-4
© Peter Collin Publishing Ltd

Communicative crossword 3   sheet A

Puzzles & Quizzes

This crossword is not complete: you have only half the words. The other half are on sheet B. Check that you know the words in your crossword. Then work with a partner who has sheet B to complete the two crosswords. Follow these three rules:

1 | Speak only in English.

2 | Don't say the word in the crossword.

3 | Don't show your partner the crossword.

`What's 1 across?'

→ **Across,** ↓ **Down**

¹T	²E	L	³E	S	A	⁴L	E	⁵S		6	
	X					E		7			
⁸C	H	A	R	⁹T		A					
	I			A		D					
	B		10	I		E					
¹¹P	I	X		L		R					
	T			O			¹²C				
		14		R			L				¹⁵E
							U				N
¹⁶P	R	O	B	I	¹⁷N	G	¹⁸B				D
		¹⁹E	X	T	E	N	S	I	V	E	

Based on the **Dictionary of Marketing**
ISBN 0-948549-73-4
© Peter Collin Publishing Ltd

41

Communicative crossword 3   sheet B

This crossword is not complete: you have only half the words. The other half are on sheet A.
Check that you know the words in your crossword. Then work with a partner who has sheet
A to complete the two crosswords. Follow these three rules:

1	Speak only in English.
2	Don't say the word in the crossword.
3	Don't show your partner the crossword.

> `What's 1 across?'
>
> → **Across,** ↓ **Down**

Based on the **Dictionary of Marketing**
ISBN 0-948549-73-4
© Peter Collin Publishing Ltd

Marketing crossword 2

All the answers in this crossword are connected with marketing.

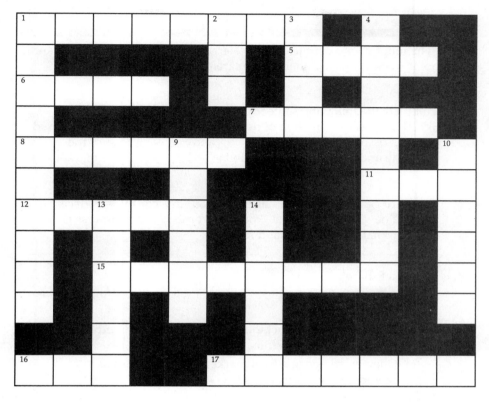

Across

1. Fixing a high price for a product in order to achieve high short-term profits
5. Symbol or design or group of letters used by a company as a distinguishing mark on its products and in advertising
6. To make as much profit for as long as possible from a particular product or service
7. beginning
8. expensive thing which is not necessary but which is good to have
11. empty space
12. general way things are going
15. high _____ = strong force by other people to do something
16. final point or last part
17. movement of passengers or goods on the way to a destination

Down

1. added to regularly over a period of time
2. Independent Television Commission
3. a _____ of produce = too much produce, which is then difficult to sell
4. total, with everything added together
9. trade in vouchers or stamps for a special free gift or a reduction in price
10. sales _____ = quality which makes customers want to buy
13. to increase or to get bigger or to make something bigger
14. main or original

Based on the **Dictionary of Marketing**
ISBN 0-948549-73-4
© Peter Collin Publishing Ltd

Quiz

How many of these questions can you answer?

1. "The four Cs" is a simple way of referring to the four most important points regarding customers - what are these points?

2. Complete the following sentence.
   SWOT analysis is a method of developing a marketing strategy based on an assessment of the _____ and _____ of the company and the _____ and _____ in the market.

3. There are generally several stages involved in a consumer's decision to buy a new product. A well-known acronym for this process is AIDA . What does AIDA stand for?

4. Is 'market share':
   a) a group of consumers in a market who are definable by their particular needs;
   b) the sales of a product that should be achieved with the right kind of marketing effort; or
   c) the percentage of a total market which the sales of a company's product cover?

5. Brand loyalty involves the inclination of a customer to keep buying the same brand of product. True or false?

6. What is a 'consumer profile'?

7. Explain the difference between classified advertisements and display advertisements.

8. A loss-leader is an article that is sold at a loss, for a purpose. What is that purpose?

9. Fads have a long life cycle. True or false?

10. What is Brand X?

Extension. Work with a partner and write a marketing knowledge quiz. Make sure you know the answers. Then ask the questions to another pair of students in the class.

Based on the **Dictionary of Marketing**
ISBN 0-948549-73-4
© Peter Collin Publishing Ltd

Communicative crossword 4   sheet A

This crossword is not complete: you have only half the words. The other half are on sheet B. Check that you know the words in your crossword. Then work with a partner who has sheet B to complete the two crosswords. Follow these three rules:

1 | Speak only in English..

2 | Don't say the word in the crossword.

3 | Don't show your partner the crossword.

`What's 1 across?'

→ **Across,** ↓ **Down**

Communicative crossword 4   sheet B

This crossword is not complete: you have only half the words. The other half are on sheet A. Check that you know the words in your crossword. Then work with a partner who has sheet A to complete the two crosswords. Follow these three rules:

1 | Speak only in English

2 | Don't say the word in the crossword.

3 | Don't show your partner the crossword.

> `What's 1 across?'
>
> → **Across,** ↓ **Down**

Based on the **Dictionary of Marketing**
ISBN 0-948549-73-4
© Peter Collin Publishing Ltd

Vocabulary Record Sheet

WORD	CLASS	NOTES Translation or definition, example...

Answer key

Word-building

Word association 1: missing links *(p.1)*

1. trade   2. purchasing   3. product
4. price   5. line   6. date

Word formation: nouns *(p.2)*

Exercise 1.

1. acceptance   2. agreement
3. classification   4. decision   5. deletion
6. delivery   devaluation   8. estimate
9. forecast   10. modification   11. offer
12. promotion   13. publicity   14. selection
15. trade

Exercise 2.

1. Our promotion of this product will involve offering customers a free gift.
2. We have reached an agreement on the budgets for next year.
3. His estimate of costs was £1m.
4. The company does not trade with the US.
5. They took the decision to appoint a new managing director.
6. The product has lost market share and is a likely candidate for deletion.
7. We have made our selection of items that are to be reduced by 25%.
8. This company offers free delivery.
9. Audiences were small because the play had not had proper publicity.
10. The refrigerator had modifications before it went into production.
11. The economists' forecast is for a fall in the exchange rate.
12. The press reported on the government's devaluation of the dollar by 7%.
13. We have received his letter of acceptance.
14. She made an offer of £10 a share.
15. What's the classification of these papers?

Two-word expressions *(p.3)*

1. junk mail
2. assembly line
3. batch number
4. blind testing
5. colour supplement
6. commercial break
7. horse trading
8. disposable income
9. lead time
10. direct marketing
11. rate card
12. brand X
13. mailing list
14. purchasing power
15. directive interview

Plural formation *(p.4)*

1. emporia   2. trade fairs   3. media
4. middlemen   5. branches   6. maxima
7. curriculums vitae/curricula vitae   8. sachets
9. consortia   10. admen   11. indexes/indices
12. periodicals   13. objectives   14. saleswomen
15. commercial agents

Word formation: adjectives *(p.5)*

1.   He showed me documentary evidence.
2.   These goods are exchangeable for those items.
3.   There are seasonal variations in the sales patterns.
4.   The report mentioned that the currency markets are currently stable.
5.   She is a divisional director.
6.   We have appointed a very experienced sales director.
7.   The agencies operate within a self-regulatory framework.
8.   Economic development has been relatively slow in the north, compared with the rest of the country.
9.   The economy is in an inflationary spiral.
10.   All industrial sectors have shown rises in output.

Word association 2: partnerships *(p.6)*

Exercise 1.

1. manage property   2. lose customers
3. freight goods   4. forfeit a deposit
5. exchange contracts   6. effect a payment
7. penetrate a market   8. debit an account
9. release dues   10. meet a target

Exercise 2.

1.   We should meet our target of £2m for turnover this year.
2.   They've been losing customers because their service is so slow.
3.   They want to penetrate the US market.
4.   We freight goods to all parts of the USA.
5.   I shall get the accountant to effect the payment immediately.
6.   The company manages property in south-west London.
7.   His account was debited with the sum of £25.
8.   I decided not to buy the item and forfeited my deposit.
9.   We are due to exchange contracts this week, so should be in our new home shortly.
10.   Now that the book is in stock, we can release dues.

Opposites 1: prefixes (p.7)

Exercise 1.
1. *un*limited   2. *in*visible   3. *in*direct
4. *un*profitable   5. *un*fair   6. *in*stability
7. *un*controllable   8. *un*favourable
9. *ir*revocable   10. *un*load

Exercise 2.
1. invisible   2. irrevocable   3. unload
4. instability   5. unfair   6. indirect
7. unfavourable   8. unlimited
9. unprofitable   10. uncontrollable

Word formation: verbs (p.8)

Exercise 1.
1. accept   2. adapt   3. adopt   4. advertise
5. agree   6. approach   7. confirmation
8. decide 9. discount   10. install   11. integrate
12. launch   13. modify   14. nullify
15. patronize   16. permit   17. select
18. subsidize   19. trade   20. turn over

Word association 3: mind maps (p.9)

1. fly-posting   2. press   3. planning
4. billboard   5. advertising rates
6. advertising control   7. legislation
8. poster   9. advertising medium
10. rate card

Parts of Speech

Nouns (p.10)

1. prototype   2. campaign   3. venue
4. shopping   5. researcher   6. chain
7. presentation   8. trend   9. image
10. briefing   11. brand   12. life-style
13. enterprise   14. catalogue   15. portfolio
16. reach   17. commission   18. quote

Adjectives (p.11)

1. immediate   2. cosmetic   3. seasonal
4. frequent   5. boxed   6. false
7. limiting   8. normal   9. reciprocal
10. nationwide   11. socio-economic
12. exorbitant   13. fragile   14. inferior
15. imperfect   16. co-operative
17. refundable   18. extensive

Verbs (p.12)

1. guarantee   2. report   3. price
4. brief   5. target   6. budget
7. research   8. distribute   9. sponsor
10. select   11. insert   12. relaunch
13. buy   14. advertise   15. sample

Verbs: past tense ~ regular verbs (p.13)

1. shifted   2. accessed   3. set
4. analyzed   5. handled   6. expressed
7. packed   8. displayed   9. transported
10. pioneered   11. adopted   12. posted

Verbs: mixed tenses (p.14)

1. reach   2. recorded   3. promoting
4. approved   5. maximize   6. switch
7. undersold   8. tipped   9. outbid
10. competing   11. expand
12. outselling

Phrasal verbs (p.15)

1. hived off   2. giving away   3. branched out
4. broken up   5. account for   6. marked up
7. put down   8. run down   9. made out
10. call in   11. setting up   12. cashed up

Adverbs (p.16)

1. The project is not *commercially* viable.
2. The contract is *legally* binding.
3. The company is *financially* sound.
4. The computer *accurately* forecast that sales would drop in the second quarter.
5. He updated the database *voluntarily*.
6. The deal was negotiated *privately*.
7. Their products are *competitively* priced.
8. The photocopier is *frequently* out of order.
9. The job was advertised *internally*.
10. We deal *directly* with the manufacturer, without using a wholesaler.

Prepositions (p.17)

1. We have a file of press cuttings ~~over~~ ∧ our rivals' products.   *of*
2. Both consumer markets and industrial markets have been affected ~~through~~ ∧ the recession.   *by*
3. The company will start work ∧ the project next month.   *on*
4. We are short ~~by~~ ∧ staff.   *of*
5. Profits were distributed ~~at~~ ∧ the shareholders.   *among*
6. These prices have been marked up ∧ 10%.   *by*
7. He received confirmation ∧ the bank that the deeds had been deposited.   *from*
8. We offer ~~to~~ a nationwide delivery service.
9. We plan to build a factory ~~to~~ ∧ the Far East.   *in*
10. The marketing director's brief was to increase coverage ~~through~~ ∧ at least 10%.   *by*
11. The company spends ~~at~~ thousands of pounds on research.
12. Consumers are found to be especially influenced by the tastes and opinions of those ~~per~~ ∧ their peer groups.   *of*
13. They have agreed the budgets ~~over~~ ∧ next year.   *for*
14. Please send me literature ~~to~~ ∧ your new product range.   *about*

Pronunciation

Word stress (p.18)

Group A: packaging, marketing, strategy, company, customer, satisfied

Group B: permission, department, objectives, expansion, prospecting

Group C: patentee, guarantee

Verbs & nouns (p.19)

	noun/verb	❶②	①❷
1.	verb		x
2.	noun	x	
3.	noun	x	
4.	verb		x
5.	verb		x
6.	noun	x	
7.	verb		x
8.	noun	x	
9.	verb		x
10.	noun	x	
11.	noun	x	
12.	verb		x
13.	verb		x
14.	noun	x	

Present simple (p.20)

Group A: inserts, takes, tests, regulates, collects, reports, packs, markets

Group B: buys, agrees, delivers, deals, falls

Group C: dispatches, faxes, advises, researches, manages, charges, advertises, produces

Past simple (p.21)

Group A: launched, shipped, faxed, financed

Group B: publicized, called, opened, organized, charged, mailed

Group C: traded, exported, budgeted, marketed

Vocabulary in Context

Marketing metaphors (p.22)

1. campaign: series of co-ordinated activities to reach an objective
2. flood: to fill with a large quantity of something
3. target: thing to aim for
4. battle: fight
5. capture: to take or to get control of something
6. saturate: to fill something completely
7. territory: area visited by a salesperson

8. blitz: marketing campaign which starts at full pressure (as opposed to a gradual build-up)
9. launch: to put a new product on the market (usually spending money on advertising it)
10. tactic: step or move involved in carrying out a strategy

Categories: the four P's (p.23)

Product: line extension, brand name, guarantee, packaging, quality control, product design

Price: competitive pricing, price list, manufacturing costs, quantity discount, payment on delivery, credit account

Promotion: commercials, free sample, mailshot, advertising, sponsor, publicity campaign

Place: warehousing, point of purchase, transportation, retail outlet, distribution channels, inventory

Odd one out (p.24)

1. *yellow goods:* the others are faster selling goods
2. *depth interview:* the other interviews use preset questions and follow a fixed pattern
3. *customer:* the others are all jobs
4. *consumers:* the others are groups within the VALS segmentation system
5. *sell:* the others refer to getting things
6. *economical:* the others refer to high costs and prices
7. *offer:* the others are what you do when you want to receive something
8. *domestic:* the others refer to countries other than your own
9. *hotline:* the others are related to personal selling
10. *by-product:* the others refer to money
11. *tannoy:* the others relate to poster advertising
12. *frequently:* the others are types of periodical
13. *international:* the others refer to the country where a company is based
14. *closing date:* the others refer to dates on a food packet

Opposites 2 (p.25)

Exercise 1.

1. buy   2. loss   3. horizontal   4. positive
5. lose   6. early   7. upturn
8. down-market   9. homogenous
10. recession

Exercise 2.

1. sell   2. horizontal   3. positive
4. profit   5. late   6. upturn
7. homogenous   8. open   9. recession
10. win

Abbreviations (p.26)

1. Value Added Tax
2. new product development
3. guaranteed homes impressions
4. unique selling proposition
5. electronic point of sale
6. public relations
7. letter of credit
8. advertisement
9. research and development
10. knockdown
11. manufacturer's recommended price
12. direct marketing
13. or near offer
14. account
15. recommended retail price
16. point of sale
17. Office of Fair Trading
18. point of purchase advertising
19. cash on delivery
20. just-in-time
21. fast-moving consumer goods
22. opportunities to see

Flow charts (p.27)

1. advertising brief >>> media planning >>> advertisement >>> advertising campaign
2. attention >>> interest >>> desire >>> action
3. manufacturer >>> wholesaler >>> retailer >>> consumer
4. concept >>> idea testing >>> design >>> development >>> testing >>> manufacture >>> distribution >>> launch >>> selling
5. launch >>> growth >>> maturity >>> decline

Telemarketing (p.28)

1. concept   2. customer   3. products
4. sectors   5. targeted   6. incentives
7. update   8. sales   9. mailshot
10. canvass   11. calls   12. handle

Promotional tools (p.29)

1. catalogues - publications which list items for sale, usually showing their prices
2. leaflets - sheets of paper giving information, used to advertise things; fliers - promotional leaflets
3. posters - large eyecatching notices or advertisements which are stuck up outdoors or placed prominently inside a store
4. advertorials - text in a magazine, which is written not by the editorial staff but by an advertiser
5. radio ads - commercials on the radio
6. television ads - commercials on the television
7. classified ads - advertisements listed in a newspaper under special headings (such as 'property for sale' or 'jobs wanted')
8. semi-display ads - advertisements that have some of the features of display advertisement (such as borders and their own typeface or illustrations), but which are printed on the classified advertisement page

Agency awards (p.30)

1.c)   2.e)   3.d)   4.a)   5.b)

Designing sales literature (p.31)

1.b)   2.b)   3.a)   4.a)   5.a)   6.c)   7.c)
8.b)   9.a)   10.c)

Talking about marketing (p.32)

1. point-of-sale   2. campaign   3. pricing
4. customer   5. domestic market   6. flier
7. giveaway   8. image   9. mailing   10. niche
11. packaging   12. catalogue   13. discount
14. promote   15. advertising   16. distribution
17. competition   18. overseas

Puzzles & Quizzes

Anagrams 1 (p.33)

1 **M** O N O P O L Y
2 **E** X H I B I T I O N
3 **S** P O N S O R S H I P
4 **S** T R A T E G Y
5 **A** N A L Y S I S
6 **G** H O S T I N G
7 **E** X P O S U R E

Word search (p.36)

A	G	C	O	P	Y	W	R	I	T	E	R
F	E	E	D	B	C	E	D	E	E	N	E
F	N	M	I	S	S	I	O	N	L	C	P
M	E	D	I	A	T	G	S	G	E	L	O
A	R	A	C	K	R	H	P	C	M	O	S
R	V	A	L	A	T	H	O	A	S	I	
T	C	H	I	P	T	E	P	R	U	T	
S	A	M	P	L	E	N	R	Y	K	R	I
O	F	F	E	O	G	E	J	E	E	O	
L	K	L	G	Y	Y	D	E	P	T	H	N
U	F	A	I	R	M	O	U	T	E	R	N
S	P	I	N	O	F	F	O	P	R	Q	R

Marketing crossword 1 (p.37)

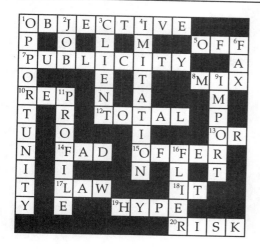

Anagrams 2 (p.40)

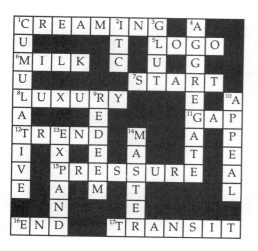

Quiz (p.44)

1. value to the Customer, Cost, Convenience for the Customer, Communication between seller and buyer
2. Strengths, Weaknesses, Opportunities, Threats
3. You attract consumers' Attention, keep their Interest, arouse a Desire and finally provoke Action to purchase
4. c)
5. True
6. Description of the relevant details of the average customer for a product or service.
7. Classified advertisements are advertisements listed in a newspaper under special headings (such as 'property for sale' or 'jobs wanted'), whereas display advertisements are advertisements in a publication which are set apart from other advertisements by each having their own typeface, border, illustration, etc.
8. To attract customers.
9. False.
10. The anonymous brand which is used on TV commercials as a comparison to the named brand being advertised.

Marketing crossword 2 (p.43)

SPECIALIST DICTIONARIES

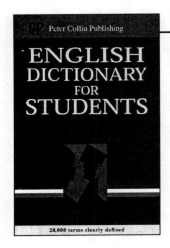

ENGLISH DICTIONARY FOR STUDENTS

A new general English dictionary written for intermediate to upper-intermediate level students. The Dictionary includes up-to-date coverage of English with over 20,000 terms, each clearly defined using a limited vocabulary of just 1500 words. Includes vocabulary used in TOEFL, TOEIC, UCLES, SAT and similar English exams.

- l written for learners of English
- l covers British and American terms
- l phonetic pronunciation
- l example sentences and quotations show usage

ISBN 1-901659-06-2   720 pages paperback   £9.95 / US$15.95

CHECK YOUR VOCABULARY FOR ENGLISH

A companion workbook of exercises, puzzles, crosswords and word games to test general English skills. Provides material suitable for students taking Cambridge First Certificate/C.A.E level exams.

ISBN 1-901659-11-9   £5.95 / US$9.95

For full details on our complete range of dictionaries and workbooks, visit our web site: www.petercollin.com or use the form below to request further information.

English Dictionaries

English Dictionary for Students	1-901659-06-2	❏
Accounting	0-948549-27-0	❏
Aeronautical English	1-901659-10-0	❏
Agriculture, 2nd ed	0-948549-78-5	❏
American Business	0-948549-11-4	❏
Automobile Engineering	0-948549-66-1	❏
Banking & Finance, 2nd ed	1-901659-30-5	❏
Business, 2nd ed	0-948549-51-3	❏
Computing, 3rd ed	1-901659-04-6	❏
Ecology & Environment, 3rd ed	0-948549-74-2	❏
Government & Politics, 2nd ed	0-948549-89-0	❏
Hotel, Tourism, Catering Management	0-948549-40-8	❏
Human Resources & Personnel, 2ed	0-948549-79-3	❏
Information Technology, 2nd ed	0-948549-88-2	❏
Law, 3rd ed	1-901659-45-3	❏
Library & Information Management	0-948549-68-8	❏
Marketing, 2nd ed	0-948549-73-4	❏
Medicine, 3rd ed	1-901659-43-7	❏
Military Terms	1-901659-24-0	❏
Printing & Publishing, 2nd ed	0-948549-99-8	❏
Science & Technology	0-948549-67-X	❏

Vocabulary Workbooks

Banking & Finance	0-948549-96-3	❏
Business, 2nd ed	1-901659-27-5	❏
Computing, 2nd ed	1-901659-28-3	❏
Colloquial English	0-948549-97-1	❏
English for Students	1-901659-11-9	❏
English for Academic Purposes	1-901659-53-4	❏
Hotels, Tourism, Catering	0-948549-75-0	❏
Law, 2nd ed	1-901659-21-6	❏
Marketing	1-901659-48-8	❏
Medicine, 2nd ed	1-901659-47-X	❏

Professional/General

Astronomy	0-948549-43-2	❏
Economics	0-948549-91-2	❏
Multimedia, 2nd ed	1-901659-01-1	❏
PC & the Internet, 2nd ed	1-901659-12-7	❏
Bradford Crossword Solver, 3rd ed	1-901659-03-8	❏

Bilingual Dictionaries

French-English/English-French Dictionaries	❏
German-English/English-German Dictionaries	❏
Spanish-English/English-Spanish Dictionaries	❏

Name: ....

Address: ....

....

...................................Postcode/Zip: ....Country: ....

Peter Collin Publishing Ltd
1 Cambridge Road
Teddington, TW11 8DT - UK
tel: +44 181 943 3386   fax: +44 181 943 1673   email: info@petercollin.com
web site: www.petercollin.com